We all have a story.

It does not define us;

it only guides us to

who we are truly meant to be.

YOU KNOW MY NAME ...
NOT MY STORY

Bianca Ozzimo

You Know My Name ... Not My Story
Copyright © 2023 Bianca Ozzimo
First published 2023

Disruptive Publishing
17 Spencer Avenue
Deception Bay QLD 4508
Australia
WEB: www.disruptivepublishing.com.au

Editing by Jandyco
Book Cover by Bianca Ozzimo
Layout by Jo Scott
Cover Image by April Werz https://aprilwerz.com

ISBN# 978-0-6455278-9-6 Print

To my beautiful family, I would not be here today

without all you have done for me.

To my brother, still in addiction.

Most of all, to MYSELF, for having the

strength and courage to keep going.

Table of Contents

Foreword

"I've finally arrived, I've made it!"

These were the first words that Bianca boldly announced to me as she nervously walked into The Soul Sanctuary in early 2022 for a 'Reiki and a Reading' with me.

As an Energy & Soul Practitioner, Psychic Medium, Published Author and Reiki Master I see so many women who feel energetically exhausted, lost and disconnected from themselves. They often come to me feeling discontent with their lives, with a desire to let go of old patterns and deep wounds, ready to reclaim their power and step into their highest soul potential.

Empowering women to reconnect and own all the parts of themselves and their feelings, even the messy, confronting parts and to honour and love themselves again is not always easy; in fact, it often feels confronting and overwhelming. However, learning to feel the feelings again and reconnect to the soul is one of the most powerful and transformational experiences a soul can move through.

Sadly, I've seen so many women come to me feeling so incredibly lost. It's little wonder, really, when we have been conditioned to ignore our feelings (which is essentially our intuition) and instead rely on our highly logical mind to guide us. So, instead of trusting our instincts, instead of trusting how we feel in a situation and acting accordingly, we find ourselves doing things we think we *have* to do rather than what we actually feel we *want* to do. At first, it might feel like the right thing to do but years of suppressing and ignoring our feelings often results in us sleepwalking through our lives.

When we are no longer guided by our feelings, which are our guiding beacon, we begin to feel discontent and disconnected from ourselves. We find ourselves morphing into people we don't recognise any more and, more often than not, people we don't actually like. As we disconnect more and more from our soul, we start to dislike ourselves, because we find ourselves not investing time, love and energy into the things that light us up and bring us joy. Gosh, we don't have the time or money for that, right! We find ourselves starting to move away from our soul's blueprint, the soul map we decided we wanted to journey on before we chose to incarnate, and that's when we start to feel sad, lost and discontented.

We feel weighted down by the heaviness of wounds and stories and the responsibility of life. We don't balance that out with joy, laughter and fun, feelings that carry a really high vibrational frequency. Our field of energy drops, and this often results in feelings of hatred towards the self (self-loathing) and wishing things were different. And for many people, women in particular, we feel like we can't change it, or we don't have the energy to change it, so we find ways to censor our feelings, we numb it and suppress it instead. We find ourselves turning to alcohol, drugs, sex, cigarettes or shopping to numb the pain. It's the comfort for the pain, and it makes it that little bit more bearable to endure.

And so, we bury it deep inside our womb space, we hide from it, we keep it a secret! But as you will come to find out in Bianca's incredible story, there is so much power and healing in speaking your truth!

After working with Bianca for over a year now, I know she shares many of my beliefs and is on a mission to empower people, particularly addicts, to speak their truth! There's something so powerful about working with someone who has deep soul experience! They have a much deeper level of understanding around what you may be feeling and the wounds that might be holding you there.

Bianca is an incredibly gifted Reiki and sound healer who moves you into a place of deep rejuvenation, healing and inner peace. She holds space for you from a deeply compassionate and understanding space, no matter where you are on your soul's journey.

Reading Bianca's book is like sitting there with her, over a cup of herbal tea, and becoming engaged and engrossed in her story as she finally speaks her truth about her rape as a 12 year-old girl, her long struggle with drug addiction and how the BDSM world broke her into submission! If you're struggling with addiction or you have a loved one struggling with addiction, *You Know My Name ... Not My Story* is a must read! It will help you to know that there is hope and give you the courage to speak your truth! As Bianca so beautifully writes:

There is another choice, there is life after trauma, there is hope after drug abuse!

Jess Sermak
Certified Life Coach, Author, Psychic Medium
and Women's Circle Facilitator

Introduction

I sit here, at age 39, and for the first time in my life I want to piece my 'fucking shitty story' together. Honestly, I have never really had an interest in my past. I had the attitude, "Meh, the past is in the past. Keep it there, none of it matters".

Well, *now* I know that's a load of crap and I realise how wrong I was. I have a strong knowing that I am meant to go back and remember my past, my story, the cruel challenging journey that has made me the woman I am today. All the addictions, abusive relationships, attempted suicides, rape—all this was not for nothing!

I now know my story isn't *just* for me and I believe that by sharing it I can give people so much hope to *just keep going*. To hold in there and keep hope alive for yourself, or your loved one. How worth it would it be to inspire, not just me, but one more gorgeous soul who is struggling? To give hope and to just know that when we are ready there is another choice, there is life after trauma, after drug abuse, and it is worthwhile to live another day.

Heck, there is life after any kind of abuse, but we must make that one decision that will make or break us. I am not saying that it will be easy. It will possibly be one of the hardest decisions you will ever have to make: *your live*, or *your die*.

Or for the people around you: *their* decision to stop enabling you and to let go, so they can stop hurting and punishing themselves. All they can do is pray and hope until you are ready to reach out to them.

And trust me when I say, "This is what we actually need you to do". I believe that anyone who has not been through the turmoil of addiction and abuse can ever fully understand its trauma. Or what it is like to have nothing and no one because of your choices, or the choices you made because of what happened to you. It really is something you need to have experienced to even begin to understand how it feels. Not only in those moments of chaos, but also during the struggle to heal and work on YOU. Yes, addictions and traumas are challenging. But you know what? So is recovery or leaving an abuser!

As long as I can remember I have always wanted to help people, I just never really understood *how* or *why*. I had a nurturing urge inside of me but helping others would mean delving back into my past. That was something I was not wanting to face, but I never imagined it would be my 'how' to help people. Quite frankly, it scared the living shit out of me to have to go back and relive all of those moments! But it was the key to me being able to understand and help people. I had to go back and remember my story to acknowledge how much I had been through, and to sit and look at the woman I am today, even after everything that has happened. Still smiling and kind, with a heart of gold.

If you have someone you love who is (or has) experiencing substance abuse, or has attempted to take their own life, or is constantly settling for abusive relationships, or is enduring any other trauma – then this book is especially for you. I hope it gives you a little insight as to why we, sometimes, make these choices.

And if *you* have survived any of these traumatic experiences and are feeling stuck, empty, alone and want a little inspiration for your journey ahead, this book is for you too.

Don't give up and never let anyone STEAL YOUR VOICE! There is so much healing in speaking your truth. You've got this, beautiful!

Chapter 1

So today, 29th May 2022 at age 39 I sit here and begin to write my story so I can truly get to know myself and be brave enough to face it head on and OWN IT. No more hiding, no more sugar-coating for others who hurt me and no more feeling ashamed, guilty or embarrassed.

Whether it is just to help me heal and grow, or this book finds its way into your hands, and you read my story, I truly hope for both of us it creates clarity and offers release. I want to give you the strength, hope, and understanding you need to take that next step into your true journey of healing.

If you are on the other side of a loved one who is currently in a life of addiction or abuse, I want this book to help you understand that 'it' is not about you. There is nothing you can do, or could have done, to change any of the choices 'we' make or made.

'It' is about us and what happened *to* us to lead us to these choices, or what compelled us to keep an abuser around, or what hurt us *so* badly we would want to take our own life. At no point during our shitty, addictive, abusive stage in life were we even thinking about you or even thinking about how we were hurting *you*. Now that may sound harsh, but it is the cold truth.

Never during my life of abuse and addiction was I thinking of how it hurt or affected anyone else. I truly want to help you to understand this. I believe that knowing this is the first step for *you* to stop self-blame.

To start with, my story may seem a little boring, but I ask you to keep reading to get to know a little of me as a child ... before my innocence was stolen from me. Then I will take you through my shitty life and the choices I made to help me survive. In some parts of my story, it may feel like there is no room to breathe, but that is exactly how it felt for me too.

For anyone who is experiencing something similar, just know you've made it this far for a reason. Heck, I wonder sometimes how the fuck I am still alive. And then I smile because I am so grateful to still be here. I know in my heart that my journey, and everything that has happened, was truly meant for me to grow and share with you. And I wouldn't change one damn bit of it! It has made me the woman I am today, and I love her exactly as she is—for the first time in my life.

When things feel a little rough sometimes, always remember: '*It's not happening TO ME, it's happening FOR ME*'. Sounds crazy right? And gosh, a long time ago I would have rolled my eyes at this and possibly sat in my space of being the victim: the '*why me*?' But now as I do the work for ME, it all makes so much sense. Yes, it is hard remembering things I had tucked away and forgotten about and tried to run away from. But as heavy as remembering it is, I am also releasing it at the same time: allowing myself to 'speak my truth' with no regret, no shame and no guilt.

Just love and forgiveness and a reminder that *'damn girl, you have experienced a lot and look at where you are now!'*

I am not ashamed of my past and I will never allow anyone else to let me feel this way either. I hope you find the strength deep within your soul to do so too. A few words I repeat to myself sometimes to help me do this are ...
I am strong, I am smart, and I am beautiful.

***

I speak very openly and authentically, and I understand that parts of my story will be triggering for some people, whether you were in addiction, or have loved ones in addiction. Please remember, at any time if you need to, reach out to someone you can trust. And, at any point if you feel inspired to *speak your truth,* I am here and I would love to listen, help, or just be there to help you find the strength and courage I know you have deep inside you.

I am also working on holding a beautiful space for you to come and talk with me personally. I would love to listen to your story and support you through this traumatic time you are going through. And I would love to help you stop enabling and/or to shift anger, self-blame, shame, and anything else that is coming up for you. I hear you, and I see you, and I feel you, and you are not alone.

You'll find details on how to contact me at the back of this book.

I am not a counsellor, nor am I a psychologist. But I am real, and I have lived through everything you are about to read and more ... a hell of a lot more! My passion is to help people speak their truth, fall in love with themselves, and blossom into their authentic self. I want you to know that, yes, it is okay to stay and live comfortably in any type of relationship, even if you aren't truly happy—if this is what you choose—but ... can I ask you to do something for me?!

Close your eyes and ask yourself:

- Do I love my life?
- Does my heart feel full?
- Is my soul on fire?
- Do the people around me lift me up and bring joy to my life?

Did you smile when you read these questions? Or did you feel unsure or even answer a straight out NO? If your answer was 'unsure', or 'no', ask yourself why? Sit with this for a while. There is absolutely no rush. Allow yourself to *feel* into why you could not answer 'yes' when you read these questions. I like to write things down as they come to me. I find it really helps and it's great to be able to go back and read what I have written.

You see, it's not selfish to want more in your everyday life, your love life, and even your career. We all deserve to feel love, joy and happiness. To smile, just because you woke up feeling so very blessed to be exactly where you are right now. To have amazing people in your life who love you exactly as you are, so *perfectly imperfect*. Sometimes in life we outgrow things, and people, and this is okay. Not everyone we meet was always meant to stay. And as scary as it feels to take the steps to make those changes to achieve what you truly deserve, I promise you it will be worth it. So, take this life and all it has to offer, and set your soul on fire!

It is now time for you to come and join me on this journey of how trauma affected my entire life, and how I managed to eventually escape and grow into the beautiful warrior I am today.

Chapter 2

I came into this world on the 14th of April 1983 in Melbourne, Australia. Born into a beautiful, loving family: two older sisters and now me. And a few years later came a baby brother which, apparently, I wasn't too happy about, ha-ha! I don't remember too much of my life in Melbourne, but I can remember my Nonna and Pop, and always lots of homemade food. With Dad's side of the family being Italian, food was a big part of our lives. And boy-oh-boy, was Nonna's cooking AMAZING! I am quite sure *no* meant *yes* in Italian. Anytime we said no to food to Nonna she would chase us with it or have it sitting there waiting anyway, lol. I remember visiting as an adult and this was still happening. No wonder we all carried a few extra kilos, ha-ha!

We lived in a small house in suburban Melbourne, and all of us kids shared one big room together. Dad was a truckie, so he was often away working, on the road. Mum stayed home to take care of us. Sometimes I would ride along with Dad in the truck, I used to think this was super fun! Back when I was growing up, we didn't have any of these electronic devices, as we do today. We would ride our bikes, climb trees and play in the backyard. On weekends we would do roller skating classes together and, boy, was this super fun! We were just getting out and doing all the things kids should be doing to have FUN.

Then, a big change happened when I was about seven years of age. Mum and Dad decided we were moving to Queensland. This meant leaving all of our friends and Nonna and Pop behind. It was super sad, but it was also exciting to be starting our new adventure.

So, we drove to Queensland: Mum, Dad, us four kids and, of course, our German shepherd, Tara. We moved into our new home, which was a lot larger than our Melbourne home. And super cool, we had a pool and OMG did we need it! Queensland was a lot warmer than Melbourne.

Soon afterwards we all started at our new schools. I can't remember why, but I was held back a year. This meant I was a little older than everyone in my grade, not that this really mattered to me. Gosh, it was so scary! A new school meant making new friends, but I found this extremely easy as I was such a bubbly little child. I loved music, dancing, arts and crafts—anything fun and creative really—it all brought me so much joy. I was such a little romantic, Mum always thought I'd be her first child married with children.

As a family, we started rock n roll dancing on weekends. *Sooo* much fun, and Mum would make us girls skirts with petticoats. They were so fluffy that when we would twirl around, they would spin right up, all pretty. My baby brother and I even entered a competition together and we came second. I remember how cute he looked in his little suit. Sometime later we started doing karaoke and it was also super fun. I loved so much to sing and dance. There was a lot more I loved to do, such as netball and ... but I won't bore you with **all** my activities, let's just say I was a very sociable, creative, romantic and vibrant little girl.

The years went by and, boy, did I miss my Nonna and Pop. We visited occasionally, but it was too expensive for us all to travel to Melbourne more frequently. We spoke on the phone often, but it was not the same as being there. And not the same as seeing them every week, as I am pretty sure we did when we lived there.

I was always a "Pop's" girl, and in my heart I still am. He became very unwell with cancer. I can still remember visiting him and seeing him with tubes hanging out of him. I was still only a child and, being Pop's little girl, it was heartbreaking to watch.

The cancer was in his throat, and as his condition worsened, he couldn't even talk on the phone properly. I will never forget the last time trying to talk with him and it didn't sound like *him*. The cancer was really affecting him, and it just broke my heart—I dropped the phone and slid down the wall in a ball, crying. I couldn't speak to him, it hurt too much. On the 22nd of January 1995 my Pop left this world. He was taken from all of us.

Mum and Dad didn't allow us to attend Pop's funeral as, apparently, Italian funerals are full-on. I was only 11 years old, and it was absolutely heartbreaking, but I guess I understood why Mum and Dad said a big, "No".

I still miss him today and writing this has brought tears to my eyes. "Rest in peace, Pop, I will love you forever. I know you are right here by my side today, and I love knowing this." I love all my grandparents, but I guess Pop was taken from me when I was too young to process it. I don't feel I ever really new *how* to grieve at such a young age, and with everything that happened after his death I am not sure I had *time* to grieve.

Not too long after this, I started smoking. I know, so young, but the older kids were doing it, so why couldn't I, right? I now believe the loss of my Pop had deeply affected me and I didn't know how to deal with losing him. Did I deliberately start putting myself in silly situations after this? Maybe.

I don't clearly remember what I am about to share with you because I shut these memories down a long time ago. I have tried to trigger a more complete recollection of the events, but I just can't. But the parts that I do remember really, really, help make sense of a lot of my future choices all the way up until today. In fact, I had blocked the memory out so, so, deep I only began to recollect it as an adult, at the age of 35. I feel I have remembered enough for me to forgive, heal and grow. And for my own heart and soul, this is all that matters.

So, not long after Pop had passed, and I must have been no more than 12 years old, I went to a party with some friends. It was a high school party, so I didn't know anyone well, but there were a few older girls there that I used to hang with.

So young, so innocent and so, so, trusting. I had no idea what was about to happen. I do not remember feeling scared, I just didn't understand what was happening. Although having blocked it out for so very long, maybe I *was* scared, ashamed or embarrassed. I can remember trees around me and sitting, leaning back on a fence. It must have been a back bush behind houses. I was with an older boy; I didn't know him, and honestly, I can't even remember how we met or how we got there. I still have many repressed memories from that night, and this is not unusual with trauma.

All I can remember of that night was we sat there, I remember him leaning in to kiss me and my pants were taken off and he had his way with me. I am not sure if he fully penetrated me—I have no feelings or visuals of this moment—but I *can* remember the strange smell of cum. I didn't have a clue back then what it was. I was just a child. Afterwards, I remember standing on the road and him telling me to wait there—and he never came back. I can see me standing there in my little black crochet top, so lost and confused, just standing there ... waiting. What had just happened and why didn't he come back?

From that moment, I never thought or spoke of it to anyone. Not one soul. I buried it so, so, deep that not even I could remember it had happened. But that night my inner light was taken from me without my knowledge, and certainly without my consent. My life went on as 'normal', except now I was making stupid shitty choices that I wouldn't have previously. The little joyful, vibrant and creative girl was slowly disappearing. I now carried a darkness inside of me that I never really understood.

It wasn't too long after that night I had my very first period. I remember being horrified and Mum trying to calm me and reassure me, "It's okay, it's just your period". Did this trigger something in me from what had happened? For two weeks after this no one could get a single word out of me. Mum had tried everything, even giving my sisters money to take me shopping, but nothing worked. Was I feeling silenced by what had happened to me? Did I feel disgusting, dirty and ashamed just as I did when I was … I guess, raped?

I have never used the word *raped,* as I always pictured rape being terrifying and brutal. And from the small, recently surfaced memories that I do have, I do not remember how it felt emotionally or physically. So, what actually happened to me? Was I raped, molested or, as I have always called it, taken advantage of? I know that no one asked for my consent, and I certainly didn't give it. I was 12 and he was a horny teenager who would have known exactly what the fuck he was doing.

Chapter 3

Starting high school was scary enough, but I also brought a lot of self-hate with me. I expressed myself through poetry, but it was no longer written with joy and love. Now it was to express self-hate. So dark for such a young girl. Being raped had really stolen my light and taken away my spirit.

I went to parties, and we'd drink excessive amounts of alcohol, smoke cigarettes, and have meaningless, unsafe sex. I think it was in year nine when I really started not to care, and I was introduced to pot for the first time. I would hardly attend school and just sit at a friend's house smoking pot and eating pizza for the day. It was like I had lost all zest for the fun, creative things I once lived for. I even dropped out of school in year nine, but Mum must have talked me into at least finishing year ten. So, I did, but I didn't attend school very often. I was already dabbling in speed, and by age 15 I had someone inject me for the first time. I wasn't using speed on a daily basis yet, just on weekends to party, but I was now using pot every other day.

Getting what, I didn't realise, was the numbness to not feel or acknowledge anything. Getting high was the only way I could feel alive from the inside out. Having no fear of what I was putting into my body or how dangerous drugs could actually be. But this thought never crossed my mind. All I needed was an escape to feel like I was alive on the inside and to be rid of the darkness I felt otherwise.

The Big Day Out in 1999 was amazing, but it was during this iconic music festival that I experienced my first acid trip. Only 16 and already putting these types of drugs into my body just to feel alive. Not too long after this, I tried acid again. I mean, I had so much fun last time, and I wanted to feel the same euphoria again. Only this time it led me to a really bad headspace. Why wasn't it working? I remember it not giving me the high, and the numbness, I expected. It sent me to a dark place; I was feeling so much anger and self-hate, and all I wanted was for these feelings to go away! This was the night I tried taking my own life.

I remember coming home and going to the medicine cupboard and taking whatever pills I could find. I wrote a suicide note and I started to cut my wrist with one of the knives from the kitchen. I then passed out from whatever I had taken and woke up the next morning with the ambulance there. I can remember the paramedic telling Mum that, if I hadn't passed out, I would have cut straight through the veins in my wrist and I wouldn't have woken up that morning.

Honestly, I don't think I wanted to die, I just hated feeling how I was feeling. I kind of just shut this away too and never spoke of it. It's happened and now we just move on, right? I mean deep down I never really knew why I used drugs and felt that way, so I just moved on with life thinking that what I was doing was fun and perfectly normal.

After trying to take my own life and thinking maybe I did have a drug problem, I reached out to Mum for help. I let her know I was injecting a lot of speed and I wanted to stop. She sent me off to stay in Townsville for a little while with my eldest sister. I'm not too sure how long I stayed there, and I did enjoy my time there, but when I came home to the Gold Coast I was straight back to using and partying. Going out all night and working all day.

Yes, I had a full-time job, I was so young, just dropped out of high school, and was working at Hungry Jacks. I loved earning money, and as soon as I was old enough to get my driving licence, I went for it. All I wanted was money and freedom and that's what I went out and got.

Well, I got what I thought was freedom. For me it looked like partying all night, coming home late and going straight to work—on a regular basis. I wasn't yet 18, but I was frequenting pubs and, sometimes, bikie bars. I had a few different groups of friends, so where I would party would depend on who I was hanging with at that time. I don't honestly know how I kept a job, but somehow, I managed to.

I never had boyfriends; I was always just *the mate* or someone to have meaningless sex with. That was until I was about 19 years old. I met him at a night club in Surfers Paradise. Let's call him Terry, shall we? We had gone home together that night and then we just kept hanging out from there. We dated for quite some time and, let me tell you, it was one hell of a ride, and not at all in a good way! All he needed was a couple of drinks and, BANG, something would switch inside him.

He was an emotionally and mentally abusive man, but he was smart. He'd never do anything abusive in front of anyone else, so people would often see me as the one that was going crazy. These days we call it gaslighting. And let me tell you that is exactly how it felt in my head, like *I* was going crazy. He'd say things to me like, "I'm going out to town to pick up some pussy". He'd be drunk, and the sleazy way he would look at me and say it, words cannot even describe.

Looking back now it was pathetic and disgusting, and why this wasn't a massive red flag for me I will never know. I guess I didn't respect or love myself, so why would anyone else bother to? So, I stayed with Terry and put up with his head-fucking comments. I lived at his place most of the time but eventually we moved into a unit of our own together.

BAD IDEA!

Of course, I see that now, but back then I thought it represented, well, love and a normal relationship. Or maybe I just wanted a man to want me, so I accepted the way he treated me. I was the good little housewife, no matter what, and I would have dinner ready for him when he got home from work. Or when he rolled in drunk at some ridiculous hour from the titty bar ... to a cold dinner.

And between the drugs and the alcohol things just got worse ...

A toxic relationship drains you of your energy, your will, and your self-esteem. The more they strip down your confidence, the harder it gets to leave. It becomes all you know, and you learn to live with it, as it slowly destroys you little by little, more and more each day.

I used to drive Terry to work every morning. One morning I just couldn't take it anymore. I can't tell you what he was going on about, or why we were arguing. All I remember is driving down the highway, and I snapped. I took my hands off the steering wheel, put my foot to the floor, and I was screaming at him.

The car crashed at high speed into a wall. How the heck I was able to open the car door, get out and walk down the highway to get away from him, is beyond me. I had no injuries, and I was in one piece! Seriously, there was an angel by my side that day because I should have died in that crash or at least had some horrific injuries.

I had cheated death a second time.

I am so, so, grateful that I am here today to be able to tell you about what happened. Naturally, I stayed in the relationship, and God only knows how I could continue to function mentally. I mean, who in their right mind stays in such a toxic relationship? Oh, that's right—ME! The relationship obviously didn't get any better.

One day, we both got into a horrible screaming match at home and things were being thrown around and smashed. It was so bad the neighbours called the cops. Of course, by the time they arrived Terry had jumped the fence and done a runner, leaving me standing there in a mess of tears looking like the crazy one. The cops took me to the police station, where I sat in a small cell and waited ... and waited. I guess this was their job, and the routine, when the neighbours were too scared to return home.

After waiting, for what seemed like an eternity, the cops came and asked me if I'd like to speak to someone at the hospital about my situation. I agreed to speak to someone. So off I went again, this time in the police car to the hospital. I remember going into a small room with someone. Yes, me the one being mentally and emotionally abused was being questioned about her sanity. But as I spoke about what had been happening to me, they could see straight through Terry's bullshit. They told me he knew every 'button' to push to do this to me. It was nice to finally have someone understand what had been happening to me.

I was released from the hospital, and I phoned Mum to come and get me. Once again, I was sent off to live with my sister and her partner, only this time she was living in Darwin. They were both in the army, so they moved around a lot. This time around, I wasn't a nice house guest. I was extremely angry, rude, and in my sister's words, "an absolute asshole".

I can't remember how long I stayed in Darwin, but when I left there, I went straight back to Terry, my abusive partner. I guess I didn't really know anything else. But as expected, his treatment of me was the same as before. Eventually even my friends, who had previously only seen me 'lose it', started to notice his manipulative behaviours. They finally saw the controlling side of him that provoked *me* to look like a crazy person. Like slyly stabbing his fingers into my vagina while I was clothed, or the demeaning things he would say to me.

So much so, I remember them one day pulling the car over and dumping Terry on the side of the road and leaving him there. It was a relief that finally other people saw why I was so traumatised. Well, one of the reasons anyway. They now saw how he was abusing me mentally and physically. But, as smart as abusers think they are, eventually the truth will come out.

Obviously, throughout this toxic relationship drugs were still involved, so I can't clearly piece everything together. But eventually I thought, "Fuck this shit!" and I left. Back to my life of partying and using speed, pills, pot and, yes, injecting. Most of the time, but not all the time. I never injected myself back then, heck, I hated needles. I always had people around me that could do it for me, even if it meant having to bribe them to into doing it.

I could be quite persuasive, especially when I wanted something. I loved the rush it would give me through my body, I loved having no awareness of any feelings, and I just loved dancing all night. It felt like freedom ... to me.

I'm sure if you've been down this pathway, you understand every word I am saying. And for me this was just getting on with life, and the only way I knew how to endure any type of pain: to self-numb with *any* type of substance.

Chapter 4

I met my second partner, Clarke, at the same nightclub I met Terry at. You'd think I would have learnt from the last relationship that this wasn't a fantastic idea, right? Ha-ha! But he was cute, he could dance, and he wanted me. Maybe I was trying to fill a void, but I was looking in all the wrong places.

Clarke wasn't all bad. We had a lot of fun together but it all still involved going out a lot and getting high. A bonus with this one was that my family loved him. He played bass guitar in a band, and I used to love watching him perform. The only downside with Clarke was that most of his bandmates were single, and when they got together and partied ... he would change. He would act like he was single but then have the nerve to get jealous at me dancing. He would physically push and pull me around like he owned me.

I remember one morning, after I had been out all night with one of my girlfriends, I went to where he was hanging with his mates, only to find some *very* young girls there with them. Clarke was in a bedroom with one very young girl bent over in front of him—flashing everything at him—and he was just watching her.

I felt anger rage throughout my entire body as I stood there and stared at him. Normally I would have lost it in a fury, but it wasn't my house to do so. I turned around and I left.

God only knows what happened after that, but he didn't follow me, he stayed there.

I couldn't go home because I was high as a kite and an emotional mess, so I went back to Clarke's house and curled up on his bed and laid and waited ... When he finally stumbled home, he was *scattered*. He'd been up all day and night drinking ... and doing whatever else they got up to.

He came into the room and pushed himself down onto me. I remember how heavy he felt, and that I didn't want to even touch him. We were face-to-face when I started to cry but he continued to have his way with me showing no remorse or any care for my welfare. I just laid still through it and cried the entire time. I never thought of it as rape then, but now I look back at it and realise if crying wasn't an indication for him to stop and get off me, then I am not sure what else would be. I was raped by my own boyfriend!

We were together for a few years, I think. I don't have a clear concept of time, as a result of using so much and having an altered awareness. Eventually we moved in together, which was exciting at the time. Despite the shitty things that happened, we had a lot of good times together, too. I guess I had already taught myself to bury the trauma and move forward ... just like nothing had happened.

I had conditioned myself this way. It's how I survived mentally, emotionally and physically. And not just in this relationship but right from when I was raped as a child. I loved to take care of Clarke, clean the house, make his lunches and have dinner on the table for him.

But even when we were trying to live a normal life, we got pulled back in to partying—and drugs were always involved. The make-or-break for me in this relationship happened when we were out clubbing one night: me and my girlfriend, and him and his mates. I was dancing away, as I did—I mean, that's what I went out for, but he hated it! He would get jealous and shove me around to stay right next to him. This time he was so rough with me, his own mate ended up punching him right in the face. The cops came and took them both away and that's the moment I made a quick exit. My girlfriend and I jumped in a limo and went back to my house, packed what we could and left. We went back to my girlfriend's house where I knew he couldn't find me. Also, I really had nowhere else to go in the state I was getting myself into. And this is when things went from bad to worse ...

***

I never really knew how to cope with the pain of breakups. So, I started using more and partying more. I had only ever taught myself how to numb the pain. Not that I had any awareness at the time that this was what I was doing. I just thought I was moving on with my life and doing what every young person did: party and have fun.

I always had someone to do this with. Someone who was just out to party for a night, or someone who was happy to use all the time with me. And if they didn't, I'd find someone who did, keeping in mind that I still needed someone who could inject my next hit for me. Until one day

I was so impatient sitting and waiting, that I did it myself. Now that I could do it myself, I had no one controlling me. No one I had to wait for and no need to share.

Now I know *no* drugs are good for you, well now I do anyway. But what I had been using for the previous, maybe, 12 years was nothing compared to what I was about to be introduced to. I call it the 'devil'. It's the one drug to me that can take anything—*and everything*—you love away from you. All of us as addicts have our own 'devil' of choice, and for me this was ICE.

I didn't have a clue what it was. I was told it was like speed, but as speed was unavailable then, I could get ice instead. I was never fearful of anything, to be honest. Which was quite dangerous! I had dabbled, okay a shitload more than dabbled, in speed, cocaine, ecstasy, fantasy and a couple of times, acid. So, what harm was dabbling in some ice, right? I WAS SO WRONG!

It all started so innocently. I still managed to hold my life together, just like I'd done in the past: using, but still being able to work and keep a steady job. But now, something was very different about using ice. It slowly got a hold of me and that's all I could think about.

I started hanging with a different crowd of people, and let me tell you, it was an *entirely* different world. Ice became something I needed, not just something I wanted. Most of the people in this world were dark, lying leeches. I didn't see this at the start because it was fun. That was until I started to have to, what's the saying, 'sleep with one eye open'? Hold on to anything valuable and keep it close. Do not trust anyone, no one is your friend.

To help you understand it better, let me describe some of the people I was engaging with. My friend would sell herself for money and drugs, and that's okay it's her choice, and at that point in my life something I did not in engage in.

I didn't sell myself for drugs, but I went along with her one day because her clients had said they'd pay us both just for me to be there. When we got there, they already had cocaine lined up for us. I remember thinking it looked a bit odd, but that didn't stop me from snorting it. I felt great, but as I sat there, I started to feel something I had never felt before and I was becoming unaware of everything.

I didn't feel right at all, and I knew something was wrong. I had to get out of there or I was about to be raped by several men. My heart still pounds as I write this. I don't know how I did it, but I got up and told my girlfriend, "Get up now, we're leaving".

One of the men stood in front of the door so we couldn't leave, and he wasn't a small man either. I must have had my crazy Italian eyes on because when I lost it and told him to move, I tell you he fucking moved! I got us in the car, and I got us out of there. Yes, silly me, I used to drive everywhere—even while under the influence.

We were close to being home to her apartment when I nodded off behind the wheel of the car, and we crashed. I believe that we had been drugged with heroin. It was the one drug I would never use by choice! We both slept for two days straight after this terrifying night. And that is a real indicator that the drug we were given was, in fact, smack.

You know, if I hadn't got us the fuck out of there I would have passed out and had all my holes raped by every man who was there. Excuse me for saying it this way, but it's the plain truth and I am certain this was what they had in mind. Thank goodness I trusted my instincts and have a fighter inside of me. Sadly, these were the type of people in my new world. There were quite a few situations where trusting my instincts and my gut feelings saved my fucking life.

Chapter 5

Now, I am not sure if it was before or after some of the events in the previous chapter, but I lost it at work one day. It had all become too much; I fell apart and asked for help. My work colleague called my Mum to come and get me and I told Mum I needed help to stop using drugs. I had asked her for help a couple times in the years previous, but never for using ice. Neither of us knew what we were dealing with.

Once again, I was back living with my parents. I was so far gone in my addiction to ice I would sneak out all hours of the night until eventually, I just disappeared. I was an ice addict and I needed it. Well, I guess any use of drugs, or other substances, is an addiction, but for me ice was so different to anything I had ever used. IT OWNED ME.

I became a different person. I quit my job, paid none of my bills and had no contact with anyone who meant anything to me. I had turned into a horrible creature, and I was particularly horrible to the people who cared about me. And still, all I was interested in was where the ice was. Little did I know, I was destroying my family.

But when you are in the grip of addiction this is the one thing that never enters your mind. Ice was so controlling that I remember literally crawling the floor one night looking for bits I may have dropped. Now that I look back at it, how disgusting and desperate is that?

Eventually, my parents packed all my clothes up and told me to come and get them. I had even become verbally abusive towards them, and I remember screaming down the phone at my dad. My gosh, I had never said a swear word to my father, before. So, I picked up my suitcase from my dad. Mum was broken, not that I knew it at the time, but she was so broken she couldn't be there when I picked up my stuff.

So, off I went with my suitcase in my car. It was just me and the devil and my so-called friends I was associating with now. To be honest, I felt nothing: I was half dead on the inside. When I unpacked, I found a letter Mum had written to me and put in my suitcase.

I may have read it, but it didn't mean much to me at that point. I was too far gone, and I just tucked it back into my suitcase.

Slowly life became harder and harder. I had someone I was constantly spending time with take, not only *my* money, but my *friend's* money too. Now remember, I wasn't working anymore, so every penny counted. I may have been an addict, but I had never lowered myself to thieving. When I became aware of what he had done, I went to find him. I was furious to find him in a pokies room, and to find he had spent every cent he had stolen. I was so angry I threw one soaring punch to his nose and sent him off his chair flying across the room. Naturally, I was kicked out of the venue, while he went and cowered in the toilet. He finally 'grew a set' and came out to the carpark, where we continued to punch on.

I was fucking tough when it came to having to defend myself, especially in the 'ice' world. I had to be street-smart. Eventually we were separated, and as I was getting into the car, he tried to push his way into the back seat behind me. Don't worry, I didn't let him in, I knew exactly what he was going to try to do: sit behind me and choke me. Call it intuition, or street-smart, or maybe a little of both.

I didn't see him again after that night, even though he was trying to track me down. You see, without him knowing, I had managed to take the money back from him that he had stolen from me. That's right! I still had his EFT card, and I remembered his PIN. I knew which day he was paid on and, as soon as I knew his pay had been deposited, I withdrew it. I took exactly what he had stolen from me. Not a penny more and not a penny less.

Understandably this started a feud between the two of us, and he was searching everywhere for me. I knew I had to hide, I was getting abusive messages and calls from him constantly telling me he'd kill me if he found me. He was also an ice addict, so I knew what he was capable of. He would have his mates try to lure me in with free drugs but, thank goodness, I'm not that stupid and I knew exactly what those people would do.

They were rapists and criminals. I'd heard the stories from the girls that had been drugged and raped by them. I had also crossed paths with a few of his enemies and I knew they'd protect me, so whenever I felt I needed to hide somewhere safe, I would go there.

To cut a long story short, it was an entire new world and slowly I found I had nothing and no one. No money— absolutely nothing. I remember feeling so frail and so hungry, but I couldn't even afford a chocolate bar. I thought about stealing one, but I just couldn't do it. I guess there was still some humanity inside of me. Although my entire life was owned by the devil, I never became a thief.

The day finally came when I just broke. I was at the absolute rock-bottom. I remember the *feeling* of that day so clearly. I was sitting on the balcony where I was living, and I couldn't stop crying. I had my Mum's letter in my hand and as I read it, I knew her words were the truth. The only words that I can remember said, "... as far as I am concerned, my daughter is dead". And Mum had included some telephone numbers for some rehab clinics in the letter, too.

I sat for so long with the letter in my hands, crying deeply. I felt so broken, so heavy, and so lost. So, I reached out to my baby brother for help. He was so upset by my circumstances, that he called Mum and Dad to tell them I had contacted him for help. Then I got a phone call or a text message from home, I can't remember which exactly. But I do remember this was the moment I was to make the biggest decision of my life, one that would make or break me. My *live* or *die*.

Because at that moment, I had planned that night to inject ice and go to a party—or I could choose for my family to come and get me. Was it a weak moment, or was I finally serious about going home and getting the help I needed? Most of me was dead on the inside, but a very small piece of me was still in there. THAT small bit of humanity still inside me said, "YES, come and get me".

Chapter 6

I still remember them pulling into the driveway to pick me up. My Mum's friend stepped out of the car, hugged me, and pulled me aside. She said I needed to be serious about getting into the car. If I got into that car, I needed to be committed to getting the help I needed because my addiction was slowly killing my mother.

Mum was not well. Her blood pressure was sky-high, so much so, her doctor was phoning her daily to check on her wellbeing. And this was all because of me. How could I do this to someone I loved? I made the choice, and I got in that car and went home. I cried a lot, but I remember walking into the house and feeling safe. I was home with people who loved me, and with their help I was going to do everything in my power to save myself.

The first step was to get me into a detox unit. I can vaguely remember parts of this long journey. I recall being assessed to confirm that I met the criteria as an addict. Obviously, I was, this hadn't been just a little bit of party fun! I can't even remember how long I was in there for, and Mum has told me I had to be sedated to keep me calm. All I really remember of it is sleeping and eating. And let me tell you after starving my body for so long, boy was I fucking hungry! I was so starved that I would eat the food of one of the alcoholics who sat next to me. The alcoholics didn't eat much in detox, so I ate for them, ha-ha! My poor little frail body, it must have weighed less than 50 kilograms at this stage. Skin and bones. Don't worry, I put the weight back on quickly enough by not using and having food to eat.

My time in detox was over, which meant the next stage of my journey was beginning: to *stay* clean. I had to secure a spot in a rehabilitation centre, so I made a phone call and had *the talk* with someone there. They don't just admit you straight away, I had to call them back in two weeks' time. I guess this was to ensure I was taking it seriously, and not just getting a quick couple of days to detox and sleep, and then take off for my next hit. Makes a lot of sense, right? If they allowed everyone in, they could run out of room for the people who are truly serious about recovery. And I definitely was serious.

During this time, my former partner, Clarke, and I were talking and trying to work things out between us. Oh, I forgot to mention we had some contact while I was using. Occasionally I would go and stay a night at his, to eat and get away and try to get money from him. He wasn't silly though; he would never give me too much money, as he knew exactly why I wanted it. I know he was a dick, but I also know he wanted me to be safe.

The two weeks waiting period went by and I was accepted into rehab. I didn't want to go, but I knew I had to. Not just for me, but for my family. It was pretty fucking scary and lonely in there! No visitors or phone calls were allowed during the first few weeks. People could leave messages or drop things off for me at the office, but that was it. The first few weeks of the treatment were when I was most vulnerable. And honestly, I hated every second of it. I felt like I was nothing like the others in there, and I only used drugs because it was fun.

I made a male friend, named Pete, while I was in rehab, so now I wasn't quite so lonely, and I had someone to chat to. In rehabilitation we had set schedules for eating, counseling, group circles and meetings. I hated all of it. I didn't believe I had any *reason* to use, I just did it for fun.

Let's remember I had no memory of what had happened to me as a child, because I blocked out most of the traumatic things that had happened to me throughout my entire life. I honestly didn't feel like I belonged there.

Everything had to be approved. For fuck's sake, I had to ask permission to take some paracetamol! Now that I think about it, it makes sense because some of the other residents in rehab had addictions to pills. A few weeks went by, maybe even three weeks I can't remember clearly, and then I had my first visit from Mum and Dad. I begged them to let me come home; I explained to them that I didn't belong in rehab. And guess what ... they said 'yes' and I was super excited to hear that.

I didn't have much of a life to go to, but I had my family. And I had my partner, Clarke, again as we were working things out in our relationship. I was all packed and ready to go when Clarke came to pick me up. I was incredibly happy to be out of rehab and going home to where I felt safe and comfortable. We swung by Clarke's house first to, you know, get a little loved-up together, ha-ha, as it was on the way to Mum and Dad's house. I was really excited, but something just didn't feel right. You know that icky off feeling you get deep in your belly when something is wrong?

We arrived at his house, and I wandered around a little. Not for long though because we couldn't keep our hands off one another. Afterwards, I walked around the house a little more. Looked in the fridge to see a cask of wine. We both knew that wasn't his wine. Was he still sleeping with the woman he had dated before me? Was he cheating on me at this critical point of my life? This was one of my most vulnerable moments, a time when I needed him most.

I didn't say anything just then, but every inch of me was saying, "Yes, he did!" I could feel it deep in my gut. And let's face it, gut feelings are rarely wrong. We got back into the car and continued to Mum and Dad's. I was *so* excited to be home! I was finally feeling safe and where I was meant to be … all except for this horrible feeling in my gut.

I went outside with Clarke for a smoke. We sat down and very calmly I asked him the question, "Were you sleeping with your ex while I was in rehab?" And, just as I had thought, and felt so deeply in my gut, the answer was, "Yes".

I remember staying calm and gently saying, "Thank you for being honest", then getting up and walking to my sister's house, which was nearby. I sat with her and just cried and cried. As I sit here and write about it and relive it all now, I can say I really had been to hell and back, and I had no more anger left in me. I was broken.

I now know that getting back together with Clarke was a big mistake, and this was the Universe protecting me. Obviously, it didn't feel that way at the time. My first night home from rehab and I was in bed with my cheating ex. I could hardly touch him or even kiss him. Honestly, I couldn't take any more pain in that moment. The only people I could allow to be in, and around, my space were those who offered me support and kindness: people I could trust.

If I wanted half a chance at recovery this was a MUST. So, I ended the relationship. How could I possibly stay with a man who could cheat on me in one of my weakest and most vulnerable times in my life? The time when I needed him, and all of him. I may have ended it but, oh my gosh, do you think I could get rid of him? He would be at my window at night, banging on it and telling me he wanted to marry me, calling me at work and sending flowers. Oh yes, I was back at my job, the same one I quit when the ice took over and I couldn't handle work anymore. My job was particularly creative: working with colour and design every day, I feel it was a good place for me to be through my recovery. But more about that later. Eventually, he got the hint that 'no' meant 'NO'.

It's funny, you know, he even popped up on Facebook ten years later asking me if we'd ever have another chance. Was he serious? And clearly my answer was a big fat NO, I politely told him to 'take care' and then I blocked him. Thank goodness he was back living in New Zealand, or I could have had a stalker on my hands again, ha-ha!

Life was a bit lonely, but I had to take each day as it came. Recovery from anything isn't easy, it is a long, hard road. Especially when you have lost everyone and everything you ever loved. Rock-bottom is a real eye-opener, let me tell you. It truly is like starting life over again, right from the beginning.

My employers had stayed in contact with my parents throughout my recovery, to see how I was doing. I loved that job, and I still do. It was creative and every day was different, and I was damn good at it—still am! And my employers knew it too! I could run the shop with my eyes closed.

I continued my recovery while trying to rebuild a life. I committed to urine tests twice a week to keep me on track, and I was living under Mum and Dad's roof again. Living with them was one of the assurances I made to be able to leave rehab. Even though being in a rehab facility wasn't for me, I still had a long journey ahead of me to recover from where I had been.

I was around 23 years old at that time and remembering that my drug use started around the age of 14, I had a very long history of using. It was not just the ice I was trying to recover from, it was *all* substance use. At that stage of my life I still felt, deep down, that I used drugs because it was fun. I would want to butt my head against a wall if someone tried to tell me that everyone uses for a reason, not for fun. I would swear black and blue that I had a great childhood and came from a great family—using drugs was all just for fun. I had repressed the memory of being raped as a child; I had buried it deep out of shame, embarrassment and fear. How could I tell anyone my WHY, when I never even knew?

Chapter 7

I started hanging out with my mate Pete (the one I had met while in rehab) as he was now an outpatient. This meant he lived in a rehabilitation house with other recovering addicts. It was a condition for him to continue in the recovery program, otherwise he would be sent to jail.

In truth, Pete was a recovering heroin addict with a life of crime behind him, so for him it was either jail or rehab. Honestly, to chat with him you would never pick any of it. He was gently spoken, funny and outgoing, and just a real kind, down-to-earth man. We just 'clicked' and got on so well that eventually our friendship became a relationship.

Pete was so very different to any other man I had been with. We connected *sooo* well sexually, and we were both clean, so no drugs were involved. Well, maybe sometimes a drink, but nothing excessive. We spent weekends away with his family and it was good, healthy, clean fun ... until it wasn't.

Slowly, Pete started to change. He would wear jumpers in the heat, disappear for periods of time, turn his phone off and keep coming up with all the excuses in the world. Yup, he had stuffed up and used. The first time it happened he asked for help, so I stood by him.

His drug of choice was heroin, which was something I didn't really understand. I remember seeing him there in bed in so much pain, and it was *sooo* hard to watch. It was the first time I actually understood what it felt like to be on the *other* end of it all. All the worry and hurt for someone you loved. That feeling of helplessness, and not being able to do anything to make their pain go away.

Pete recovered, but eventually he ended up down the same road again and the next thing I knew he was calling me from jail. Again, I was feeling helpless on the other end of that phone. I remember the feeling of panic running through my body with that phone call. He was such a beautiful man, but he just kept choosing the same wrong path.

He was now out on parole, so any use of drugs or stealing and he was back in ... and back in he went. I visited Pete in jail with his mum, and I remember having to go through all the scanners and drug testing just to get through the door. One day I tested positive for drugs—WTF!! No, I wasn't using, but apparently residue can linger in your clothes and never wash out, who knew? So, this was the last visit for me. I was done.

Having to see Pete behind a glass window was not how I wanted our relationship to be. And yes, it looks exactly like it does in the movies, so *I* felt like a criminal. I had worked too damn hard to go backwards, right? I was done and dusted, and so life suddenly became a little bit boring. Yes, I had a job and yes, I had my family, but I had no really close friends left. I mean 'the devil' (ice) had been my best friend for so long, and at that time I didn't need, or want, anyone or anything else.

I was always pretty close with my baby brother, and I started hanging out with him and his friends who, soon enough, became my friends too. It started with going down to the bowls club for drinkies, then we started heading out to the gay clubs and partying. It felt *sooo* good to dress up and dance again ... and to smile and laugh again.

Oh yes, my brother and some of his friends are gay, and boy, do I love this community! They are all such fun, and boy, can they dance! I remember eavesdropping one time to hear them organising something, and they were trying so hard to hide it from me, but if you've met me, you'd know that's impossible, ha-ha!

So, I pushed my way in, only to find them organising pills for the night. I remember my brother saying, "No!", but I didn't take no for an answer, and remember I can be pretty persuasive when I want to be. What's a couple of pills, right? Wrong. This is where it starts. With me, once again, filling every weekend with drugs and dancing—and I was loving it. Always keeping it to weekends-only, I was not ever allowing myself to go back to where I had been. I'd felt rock-bottom before, and I never wanted to feel that again. So, I partied all weekend and went to work all week.

In between all of this, my brother, me, and a few other friends, had made a couple of trips to Thailand, and it had been amazing. Eventually, my brother and I moved in together. We had both been living at Mum and Dad's, so this was FREEDOM! We were so alike, in so many ways, that it was actually quite dangerous. For a while it was just speed and pills but, sooner or later, we were smoking ice. Even though we kept it to weekend-only use, we were smoking a lot of it.

I had a 'safe' friend who would take control of my money when I felt that I was going to continue using. This would stop me from buying more drugs. I had set this up with her so I could never slip back to using every day. I still had Mum's letter tucked next to me in my drawer, and I would read it from time to time, to keep me on track.

Now I know using again, even recreational use, was not a good thing. However, for some reason it had to be a part of my journey. But let me tell you, my body new *exactly* when it was Friday and time to get it's fix. At first, I didn't even know anyone to get ice from until a friend of a friend introduced me to someone. My new dealer, it just so happened to be, was located right on the way home from work, so I'd swing by, pretty much every Friday to get my weekly fix.

This went on for quite a while—maybe months, probably more like years, who knows? And although it was all just recreational use, I was still an addict, and at any time I could end up exactly where I didn't want to be again. I don't know what came over me but one day, years down the track, I just looked around the room and had a feeling and I asked myself, "WTF was I doing? It's no longer fun and it's consuming my life!" Not using all the time gave me the chance to feel the highs, and then the massive lows, of coming down and recovering—and I was done with it!

That was it for me. I wanted something different, something better.

I will never understand what came over me, but I am so grateful I had the strength to just stop: without help, without hitting rock-bottom, just me and my own will. Life was a little different from that time on, but I still had a few friends: some who didn't use drugs, and some who did use drugs but kept me at arm's length to try and hide it. We'd still catch up for drinks, but let's face it, I've been there and knew who was still using drugs, and that's totally okay. But now it was something I didn't want around me anymore, and they knew this too. We were all on our own journey and it was never for me to judge.

Not too far down the track, these same friends kept trying to set me up with one of their mutual friends, let's call him Justin. I think I had said I wasn't ready for another relationship about ten times, but they wouldn't take 'no' for an answer. I had never really gone on a proper date, so I was pretty scared about it. I think one of the biggest fears was: how do I let someone else get to know me, when I don't even know myself? Heck, I had been an addict from age 14 until age 29—more than half my life, at that point.

Finally I gave in and said, "Okay". I'm sure I did this just to keep them all off my back. So, off we went to see a movie together. He was quite the gentleman: picked me up and dropped me home and said goodnight. No sex, no drinking or partying, just a normal evening out. Wowzahs! Who am I? Ha-ha! We continued to see each other and naturally a relationship developed, and wow, can I just say the sex together was out of this world! We really connected physically.

He trained in Mixed Martial Arts (MMA) and would fight professionally. Going to watch him compete was exciting and scary, all at the same time. I had been doing some weight training with a personal trainer at a regular gym, and occasionally would join in on Saturday boot camp. But watching him train excited me, and eventually it led me to start training in Muay Thai. There was a gym directly across the road from work, so perfect. I would finish work and go straight to training.

Muay Thai became a massive part of my life. I met some great people and, while the training was super hard, it was also fun. I'm not certain, but maybe it gave me that rush of adrenaline that I used to get from using. One thing for sure though, I do know it made my heart smile, I loved training, and it was good for me. Go figure! What a massive turn around, right?

Unfortunately, the relationship between me and Justin didn't last. He still shared a flat with his ex-girlfriend, and she was still in love with him. And she was *sooo* controlling, heck, I couldn't even sleep at his house—like what the actual fuck?! He had no balls to stand up and tell her 'NO'.

So, I was outta there! It destroyed me, but I continued to train my Muay Thai, which made my heart smile, instead of filling the void with drugs. Go me, right! I decided to do a challenge at the gym and train for a fight to get into the ring. What an achievement it was to even get over those ropes and punch on. I wasn't that great in there, because it was so scary. Everything I had learnt in training kind of just disappeared, and the adrenaline took over. But I felt like an absolute winner for getting in there and trying.

Chapter 8

Life was pretty damn great, but then I had a small slip up. I had been informed that someone from the crowd I grew up with, and used a lot with, had died. I was hesitant about whether to go to the funeral or not. I thought to myself, "You are clean, strong and fit, right? You'll be okay". So, I went and paid my respects.

After a couple of drinks at the wake—which was at a pub after the funeral—my guard was down. Before I knew it, I had made the decision to go back to the house with the old crew and the pipe was in my hand before I knew it. The 'devil' had found me AGAIN—but not for long. I pulled my head in and said, "No more. WTF was I doing? I had been going so well". I knew from that very moment on I could not, and would not, ever have it around me again. And let me tell you, I have kept that promise to myself until this day.

But unfortunately, using that *one* time disrupted my recovery and sent me backwards. I was training for another fight at the time, but I cancelled it and I turned to food for comfort.

No matter how hard I trained, I just kept eating, filling the void, and putting on weight. I did eventually train for another fight, and dropped a little weight, but after that fight my eating habit continued. I had faced drug addiction, smoking, and heck, even drinking too much. But food addiction—this was a new feel I didn't even know was possible.

All I could think about was what I was going to eat next. I still trained hard, but as they say, diet is the key to weight management, so I continued to put on more and more weight. I couldn't control it; it was like it was out of my hands. Unless you've actually experienced it, it would be easy to sit back and say, "Well, just stop eating." Well, no it is not that easy. Honestly, it's like someone saying to a drug addict, "Well, just stop injecting yourself."

I grew more and more depressed. I would hardly go out. I hated myself. One day I just fell into my Mum's arms crying, and I was an absolute mess. I weighed over 100kg and if I didn't do something about it, I would continue to eat and put on weight. This wasn't just about weight though; this was also about my mental health and my physical health. We chatted about what I was going through and that's when Mum helped me look into weight-loss surgery. My private health insurance didn't cover it, so there weren't many surgeons who would touch me, but with a bit of help from the right people we found an option.

It wasn't just a case of booking in, paying for the surgery and away you go. There was a process to go through. Firstly, I had to have a consultation with a counsellor before they would even consider me. They had to be confident that the surgery was right for me, and that I would cope with the procedure *and* the recovery. This was one of the best decisions I have ever made to help myself, and I'd do it all over again. People think it's the easy way out and that's okay for them to have their opinion, but let me tell you, it is not the easy way out! It is still goddamn hard work, and the weight can go back on just as easily as it came off. And throughout the years since my surgery, it sure did fluctuate, between an extra 10kg to 17kg put back on. The surgery does not fix the emotional attachment to food, and that was something I had to learn for myself. I think it is only just now, at this point in life, that I truly get this.

After my surgery, and the recovery from it, I got straight back into my training. The first 10kg came off easily, but the rest I had to work for. And I still had a heck of a lot of work to do within myself. Self-love and acceptance were something I had always struggled with, and even at this point in life I didn't really know why. I still didn't have a huge circle of friends, but the people at the gym were like a big family and I had my work to keep me busy too. Life after addiction is pretty much about starting all over again.

Then I came back into contact with an old friend, Dana, who I had met through my brother. So, yes, she was from my party days, but she was also on the straight-and-narrow, and she had cleaned up her life. We got chatting one day and I couldn't believe my ears. Excitement and curiosity came over me, just listening to what she was telling me about an entire new fantasy world out there. You know the ones you only read about, that possibly couldn't exist, but have you on the edge of your seat as you're reading. This lifestyle was real, it actually existed, and it was the world of all things kinky: Bondage & Discipline and Sadism & Masochism, BDSM for short.

I was gradually introduced into a *dynamic* with Dana and a man who, in time, I called 'Daddy', and he called me 'Baby Girl'. They knew my history, so as much as it was about having fun altogether, it was also about building my self-confidence. Back then, I couldn't even look at myself in the mirror and, gosh, you'd never catch me in a dress. Even though I had lost a lot of weight, I still really struggled with my body image. But this all changed, and slowly I became confident, and I absolutely loved dressing up in *aaallll* the pretties. Exploring for the first time with a man *and* a woman was something I had never even thought about, especially with a friend. But it was fun, exciting, and interesting.

As fun as our little dynamic was, I had learnt about *parties* etc., and I was *sooo* eager to get out there and explore them. Dana and I couldn't do this in the dynamic we were in with 'Daddy' so ... we left. I remember our first party; we were so nervous. Dana and I didn't know what to expect or even how to dress for that type of thing. But going along was a big eye-opener and it really helped us to connect with the BDSM scene. I met new people and started finding myself, and who I was, in this exciting new world.

I was cheeky, fun, and sparkly and my BDSM name was Princess Brat. I loved to dress up in tutus, sparkles and anything shiny, short and pretty, and I loved to be the centre of attention. I was never one to dabble my toes in the water—so I was straight in there to try everything. I soon figured out that extremely heavy impact was my choice of play, and yes it was okay: all was consensual and safe. I was cheeky and giggly, and no one could break me. I became quite well known for this and I loved to put on a show and give people a challenge. I had met a lot of people in the scene, and I was very well looked after, and looked out for.

The BDSM world isn't just about kinky sex and a little whip, it honestly helped me grow, and it taught me to love myself and the body I am in, how to have patience, and how important communication is in normal life and in the BDSM scene. This new world of all things I desired had opened me up, and I had never felt so strong, confident, and alive as I did right then. I can't really explain it properly, but I was on a high without using any type of substance.

I felt beautiful inside and out. Little did I realise this was actually my new addiction: my new drug, my new need, and my new place to hide. I was being beaten black and blue, and not actually feeling any physical pain, so I was now using pain to rid my own hurt and fill any remaining voids.

Chapter 9

Life felt pretty amazing now. I was connecting with new friendships, both sexually and non-sexually, and I was exploring this beautiful world on so many different levels. In time, I entered into a new three-way dynamic with Dana and another man, named Harley, who I had met through chatting in the scene. We were all pretty open-minded and we explored things I never thought I would try or even knew existed. The sexual chemistry between us was out of this world, but I won't go into too much detail here. I will let you tap into your deepest, darkest desires and use your imagination ... after all I'm not here to write a sex story, ha-ha!

It was all super amazing ... until it wasn't. I am not saying I was perfect in all of this, heck, I still had my little emotional moments learning how to share, and so on. But I will say, I never deserved what happened to me in any way, whatsoever. Looking back now, I make sense of it by knowing that *'it's happening FOR us, not TO us'*.

Anyway, Harley's ex was in the scene, and for some reason, she did not like me, in fact she was extremely jealous of me. I will have to guess she still had feelings for this man.

Her name in the BDSM scene was Poison Ivy and let me tell you, she was actually evil, nasty and poisonous. If I am being honest, that name suited her perfectly! Even though it was me and another woman in the dynamic with Harley, she only had it in for me. I will never quite understand why, but it was like her only mission was to fucking break me down and get me out of the way. And she sure did. I found out that Harley had lied to me about staying overnight at Poison Ivy's house, so *her* behaviour and *his* dishonesty broke me down. A lie is a lie; and lies don't sit very well with me. Yes, I may not have liked it if he had been honest with me, and I may have reacted to it, but at least I could have dealt with it in my own way.

Poison Ivy started sending me brutal messages, but I held back from retaliating to them, as I knew this was exactly what she wanted. Even so, it broke every bit of my spirit and the dynamic that we had thought was rock solid. Well, Harley used to tell me that she would never come between the three of us, that he'd be stupid to let that happen as he knew how lucky he was. But all this was gone for me, the trust was broken and so were we.

My girlfriend Dana and I had always had open and honest communication in our relationship, and if someone wanted to continue to play with someone from the broken-up dynamic we would always check in with one another first. She had actually helped to teach me this as we entered into the new world. And I had put all of it into play with our last dynamic: checking-in before even thinking about playing with the last man we had left, seeing how it would make her feel, and if she was okay. So, I guess I just thought this was the right thing to do, and if the tables were turned that she would do the same thing out of respect for me.

Unfortunately, I found out on a few different occasions, that they were still playing together and keeping it from me. I won't delve into how I found out, but I did, and it was not from either of them. For me this was not okay. It was hurtful and it broke my trust with them.

Yes, it was okay for them to continue playing, of course it was. And yes, I probably would have been hurt had they approached me about it beforehand. But at least I would have had the chance to cope with it in my own way, and it would have been a hell of a lot easier to deal with than the way I had found out about them.

Through all of this, I was going for a follow-up appointment with my hypnotherapist. Previously, Dana and I had been for our first session to quit smoking, and it was working a treat. So, just to make sure I could keep up the good work, I thought I'd have a touch-up session. I was sitting in the waiting room for my appointment—and in it came, a haunting memory.

This is where I had the very first memory of the past, a vision, a flash-back of what had happened to me and what I had buried so deeply inside of me for over 20 years, until then. 2017 was the year I remembered that I had been raped as a child. I have said before that I don't recall being scared, just so confused as to what the fuck was happening. But why had I blocked it out so completely that I never remembered it had happened until that very day?

I went in for my session and I told him about my memory. We decided to make that session about healing the little girl inside of me. Telling her that it was okay now, and that she was safe, and it was not her fault. I am going to say it really helped me as I didn't feel ashamed, or scared, or even that it was my fault. I just know it happened and fuck me, it explained so goddamn much of WHY I used drugs, WHY I turned into a moody and angry little girl, and WHY I hated myself.

You know, it's possibly even why I continued to choose emotionally unavailable men, and why I also struggled so much with the breakup of a toxic relationship. Did this make me feel abandoned just as I did when I was told to wait on the road after I was raped? I mean, my family and I never really understood why I used and chose the pathway I did. But now it all made so much sense. I truly believe my exploration in the BDSM world, and all my heavy play, helped me heal and possibly helped me to open up and remember.

I continued to explore the BDSM world, but not in a dynamic this time. I was just getting out to parties, meeting people and making new friends who are still in my life today. Deep down, I believe I had put up an emotional wall to stop anyone getting too close to me. Now sitting here and thinking back, I had been through a lot and with my recent memory of my past on top of it all, I was protecting myself from any more hurt and heartache.

I had a lot of great friends, but that very same year an especially dear friend came back into my life. Many years ago, we had gone our separate ways, but when we reconnected, it was like we had never been apart. We trained Muay Thai together and even did a trip to Thailand and trained there—what an experience that was. It was *sooo* hard training in the heat! I know I definitely wasn't prepared for it, ha-ha!

Life was still pretty great, and I had some amazing people in my life through the BDSM scene and Muay Thai. However, I was drinking on the weekends again, and looking back, it was all probably a little too much without being aware of some of the self-numbing this involved. But we do not realise these truths at the time, at least not while we are still sitting within all of our emotions.

Chapter 10

After about four years in the BDSM scene, I slowly lost all desire for all the usual play I used to enjoy. I had enjoyed some pretty heavy play throughout my years and, of course, it was all consensual. I was one cheeky, fun, hardcore little brat that no one could break, until one night ... it was interrogation themed, so it was pretty heavy play. This was right up my alley. After around three hours of being beaten with bats and other implements, being bitten, having pegs attached to my private parts and then whipped off, being waterboarded, gosh the list goes on, and for the first time ever ... I broke, used my 'safe' word and just cried.

I believe this was the moment where I started to heal. Gradually, I didn't enjoy the pain anymore and I felt ready for something real in my life: a real connection with someone. There was a lot going on at work, too. After 14 years with my employer—including times where I left and then returned to the job—I was starting to break.

Now, I know how much they must have genuinely cared for me to have supported me in my days of using and getting clean again. But the owner, well he really was from another generation, and he believed that you should be scared of your boss. He would work all of us staff members against one another, and then follow me around with so much negative talk about everyone. And gosh, it was so, so, draining!

The workplace had become totally toxic, and I was being worked to the bone. Fuck, at one stage, I worked seven days a week for almost two years! If I wasn't at the workplace, I'd be having meetings or doing reports at home. For what? Living like a robot! I had reached out to my boss face-to-face, via email and via text messaging to express how I was feeling, and I was ignored. My anxiety was through the roof. I was seeing my doctor on a regular basis because my body was no longer able to function properly. It had been screaming at me for so long and I just kept ignoring it and pushing it all to the side—as I do.

I was on anti-depressants to deal with my symptoms: heart palpitations, anxiety, vertigo, and now my hair was starting to fall out, the start of alopecia. The doctor recommended I take a week's stress leave and to really consider getting out of that workplace, as it was destroying me. So, after numerous times of reaching out for help with no response, and a week's stress leave, I finally handed in my resignation, and I left. I learnt the hard way how important a work/life balance is.

Now, where was I? That's right, I was having a break from the kink life, no more parties, etc., I was ready to just 'be' and open my heart to someone and, yes, one man only. I was ready to find the love of my life and build a life together with him. I didn't have a clue who he was yet, ha-ha, I just knew I was ready for more.

I wrote a little list and tucked it away in my drawer. I was appealing to the Universe for a few things:

- Travel
- Financial freedom
- A man who was financially stable and who could be my best friend

I had a few other things on the list, but I cannot remember exactly what they were.

Anyway, years went by, and I was now sharing a house with George, a male friend of mine who I had met in the kink scene. May I add, he was the best housemate ever! I still had a lot of friends who I had met in the scene, and who are still my friends, but I wasn't attending parties and I no longer had a desire to be beaten black and blue.

George hosted a barbecue at the house, one day. Now, he didn't just cook *any* barbecue, this was the real deal! He'd be up all night smoking brisket and ribs, making cornbread and coleslaw—the works! It was *sooo* goddamn good! I was pretty hung over on this day, as I had been at a 40th birthday party the night before. And boy, was that a night to remember, and not just for me either, but I won't kiss and tell, he-he!

Anyway, George had his mates over to test his barbecue, and there was me: on the couch half dying, with George bringing me food. He was always good like that. I remember one of his mates especially, I may have been dying but my man-radar was still on, he-he. He had a nice clean cut beard, and he was wearing a white t-shirt and denim jean shorts. I liked what I saw, so for the next few weeks I was at George to find out if his mate was single or not ... on the sly though. Not long after this, George had a spot participating at a barbecue festival, so a heap of us went along to help him. And, yup, this new man, Shane, was one of them. Yes, I was super excited to work at the barbecue festival, and even more excited that he was going to be there too, and this time I wouldn't be half dead on the couch.

OMG what a day, it was *sooo* busy, I think we served about 500 meals in four hours, and we killed it! Definitely a successful day, *and* I got to connect a little with the man I had my eyes on! He was outgoing and sociable, and well, I thought he was very handsome from the first day I had laid eyes on him. I don't think he even picked up that I was flirting with him, and I think he thought George and I were 'together' because we were always cuddly and friendly with one another.

I can see how it possibly threw off this vibe, but I am cuddly and friendly with most of my friends. I built up the courage to find him on social media and send him a message. I wrote something along the lines of, "Would you and your beard like to catch up for coffee?", and he actually said yes. From that moment on we chatted all day, every day, right up until we had our first date, which wasn't coffee.

We grabbed some drinks and sat by the fire at his house. It was perfect, we chatted all night until about 3:00a.m. and we just seemed to be on the same page about everything. I never really did do the 'date thing' in my past, but here I was, killin' it, ha-ha. A date with a man who seemed to have his shit together: nice house, his own business, a great sense of humour, and he could hold a conversation. We continued to text each other all day and night, and when we caught up, we just connected well every time.

No phones, no tv, just food and conversation. I remember the feeling of excitement rushing through my body, and the butterflies I would have in my stomach, every time before we caught up, and the feeling was mutual. Until he told me he couldn't do this anymore ... Confusion rushed through my head, and all I could think was, *"This doesn't make sense!"* and then I was pushing at him asking, "Why?"

I knew Shane felt the same way I did; I could feel it in his energy, in the way he kissed me, and in the way we talked. So instead of listening to his words, my entire soul listened to his actions. I was in such a good place in life, I remember telling him I had enough love in my heart for the both of us, until he was ready. He was so different to any other man I had ever been with, and he was worth holding this space for, for the both of us, until he was ready. We clicked in a way I cannot adequately put into words, and for the first time my guard was down, my heart was open like never before, and I was my true self. And my entire being knew he felt the same way, but why was he scared? What had happened to him to make him this way with a woman?

Shane hadn't had the most loving partners in the past. They sounded like, what we might call, gold diggers—only interested in taking his money. I could really understand how this would put a man's guard up, so I did everything in my power to show him that I was nothing like the women from his past. As much as he tried to pay for everything, I insisted that we share and take turns. I believe it should be a two-way street and I do not like to 'take' all the time—I need to 'give' too. So, we shared. Almost three months in and we were in love! I had fallen head-over-heels for this man, and I know the feeling was mutual. I can still remember the first time he looked at me and told me he loved me, like it was yesterday. And I remember sharing all of this with my Mum, telling her he was *the one,* I could just feel it.

We spent our weekends trying out new places to eat, sitting by the fire, out on the jet ski or on little road trips, always doing something fun and enjoying one another's company. We were living and we were doing it together. I can sit here now and close my eyes and feel him draw closer behind me, wrap his arms around me, and tell me, "What a good team we are together." Then he would kiss me for no reason other than he loved me, he loved us. My heart was full, and I wanted this to last forever ... until the cracks started to show.

Now I sit here, and I want to speak my entire truth, but at the same time I am trying to be gentle with my words. After everything that happened, Shane is still a good human with a good heart, he just has a lot of self-work to do, and that is something I cannot help him with. And as much as I did try to guide, lift, and support him, it slowly drained and depleted every inch of me, and all my self-love in doing so. I didn't realise it, but I was giving so much without receiving it back in the ways I needed. A person can only be pushed away so many times. And, as I have already shared with you, it was never like that at the beginning of our relationship. I felt 'seen' and loved ... until I didn't. Until I had to actually start asking if he was attracted to me, and if he loved me.

Chapter 11

It all started with a little lie. To this day, I don't think he sees it as a lie, or even has any understanding of how it affected me. Now, we know I am pretty in touch with my intuition, and every inch of my gut was telling me there was something he was not telling me. He had recently taken an interstate trip to Melbourne; I stayed home as I had commitments, and he didn't actually ask me to go with him. I could feel in my belly he was skipping over telling me some of the details about the trip. I had given him multiple opportunities to be honest with me, but he continued for weeks to choose to push past it and say nothing.

Now, if you know me, you'd know I can't just let this go until I investigate a little further, so I continued to prod. Not in a nasty, pushy way, just in conversation giving room for it to come up. I knew he was keeping something from me, and this was not okay. And I knew this from the time he was in Melbourne. I could feel it, and I could also tell by the messages he had sent me. After all, we had been together for three months, so any pattern of change in behaviour felt obvious to me. He eventually cracked and, of course, I was right.

In Melbourne, he stayed at his ex-partner's home the first night he got there. He didn't tell me, as he didn't want to cause any confrontation between us. But I didn't feel like this was the entire truth and I couldn't quite shake the feeling I had in my belly. So, I re-read all the messages from when he was in Melbourne. I wrote everything down that was trapped in my head and made space for new information. This is just how my brain works and, sure enough, I was right.

He had stayed with her *two* nights. Why, the fuck, not tell me this if nothing happened, right? He wasn't an overly sexual man, so I did believe, somewhat, nothing had happened. But then the logical side of my brain could never quite move past, 'if nothing happened, then why lie?' Now normally, at the first sign of lying I back away from people and slowly distance myself from them. And yes, these lies broke me and crushed me from the inside out.

We spoke about it, and how I felt, and he continued to tell me it was the entire truth. I had decided to work together and try to forgive him and move past it. It wasn't easy and, honestly, I tested him a few times to see how he responded to what I did.

For example, I posted a photo of us on social media, tagged him in it, and wrote a beautiful post for all our friends and family to see, all the while knowing his ex would see it too. I guess I wanted to see his reaction, and you will never fucking believe what he did. He untagged himself from the post and changed all his social media settings so I couldn't do it again.

When I confronted him about it, he told me he didn't want *her* to see it as she may try to destroy his business. Why, the actual fuck, did he say this? Did he just put her feelings before *mine*, and was he embarrassed or ashamed of being seen with me? Oh yes, she was his bookkeeper at the time, which I had been okay with ... up until NOW. Why this wasn't the red flag I needed to get the fuck out of there, I will never know!

Love does funny things to us, but I guess I was holding on tight to what we had. I expressed to him how it made me feel, and he did apologise and tell me he would do anything to make it up to me. But, honestly, at that moment I was still angry, he had seriously 'torn' me into pieces, but I loved him. Here I go again, not realising it and trying to force a future with a man who was emotionally unavailable. But as I do, I pushed it all to the side once again, and tried to move forward.

We still got out and about as we always had, but I don't think I ever truly healed from it all ... and he had changed too. But I, damn well, still gave this man every inch of my soul. He became detached, both emotionally and sexually, and no matter what I did to try and communicate and fix *us,* I felt pushed away and—what I now understand—*silenced*.

No matter what I tried, we could never get back to where we had been and, believe me, I tried everything: dressing up in sexy lingerie, where I was told to sit down and enjoy my drink; or mid-way through intimate moments, it seemed that pushing me away and folding the towels was more important. I think the one thing that really destroyed me was coming home from gym one morning to find a used cum rag on the bed. Did he really prefer to do that than touch me?

I felt embarrassed, ashamed, hurt, angry, unwanted and not good enough. I approached him about it when I found it and he denied what it was, until I kept questioning him and I got a "Sorry". Did he understand how this made me feel? I was fucking crushed on the inside! But there was me, still always telling him how sexy and handsome he was, making sure he had his lunches ready for work, cleaning his house, and the list goes on.

Let's face it, I have a very sexual and kinky background, so I knew how to please a man and how to get his attention. It's just that this one wasn't interested and none of it made any fucking sense. Never have I been pushed away from anything that was fun and sexual, especially in a relationship. The more I tried, the more I began to lose love for myself.

I was slowly closing off on the inside and shutting down the part of me that once sparkled so brightly to the world. The more I tried to communicate, the more I started to lock down from not being heard. And my body was screaming at me, on the inside, to LEAVE. I was beginning to find comfort in drinking, and each day I was waking up and pushing aside whatever had happened between us the night before. Which was usually him pushing me off or not wanting to talk, etc.

We had broken up a few times in between this, but he always told me things would change and, well, they did for a week or two, then things would slip back to as bad as they had been. Basically, there was nothing sexual and no emotional intimacy between us anymore. All we had now was getting out and about for weekends away, and all the other things we enjoyed doing. Looking back on it, without all the intimacy—emotionally or sexually—what we had was a really great friendship.

However, my entire being was shaking deep inside my belly, screaming out at me to leave. And I just continued to ignore it, to shut it out and to keep pushing, holding on to what we used to have. My body slowly started shutting down, and I didn't recognise that the two things were connected. My periods slowly became almost non-existent, with only random spotting at best. I felt so dead on the inside.

And so, every time he continued to push me away, emotionally or sexually, it destroyed me a little more. And, every time I chose to ignore it, well ... self-destruction goes on and on and on in this love story.

Chapter 12

During one of our breakups, I set myself up in a small apartment. I just couldn't take it anymore and I hated how I had become within myself. I didn't see my friends any longer, and I barely wanted to leave the house. I had become dangerously socially awkward and anxious. But here I go again, giving our relationship one *last* attempt. AGAIN ...

He was planning to talk to someone about his emotional issues and whatever was causing them, and I wanted to stand by him through all of it. Every inch of me wanted it to help us get to a better place, but it didn't. Eventually we both decided that enough was enough. After everything we had been through in the preceding 19 months, I was emotionally exhausted and closed off. I had nothing left to give. I had literally given every inch of my heart and soul to this man, only to be left broken, exhausted, and stripped of all the self-love and self-worth that I had worked so hard to achieve.

My hair started to fall out, and once again it was the start of alopecia. This was finally where I connected my non-existent periods and hair loss to my emotional stress. After ignoring my body screaming at me for so long, my body was now starting to speak to me in other ways. In ways that I would actually listen to, and fucking choose ME. I had played the *poor Shane* card for *sooo* long, now it was time for me, *poor fucking me*. It was time to fight for myself.

There would be no more going back to something that was destroying me and causing me to slip back into old habits. It was clear that my body was shutting down on me and, if I continued to keep doing what I was doing, it wasn't going to end very well for me.

I truly believe Shane is a good man, and none of what he had done was intentional. And to this day, I know that he loved me, he just never knew how to *give love* or how to *accept love*. But I now know this was not my problem to fix. He always told me I was too good for him, and he never knew what to do with me. And you know what? I sit here now, and look back and, fuck yes, I was too good for him, and I still am.

I deserve a deep lover, and for a man to share with me the exact same love that I give to him. I will be loved the way I love, and nothing less. The one thing this relationship showed me was how I can truly love, and how I could truly open myself to love. I now understand the way I want, and deserve, to be loved and to me this is fucking beautiful.

But the first thing I needed to do was fall in love with myself ... for the very first time. Before I could even think of allowing anyone in, this was a must. I mean I had just come out of a relationship where I had to *ask* if I was loved or if he thought I was beautiful. Having to do that is not okay, EVER.

And it has taken me until the age of 39 to know my worth. No more pushing things to the side. I was now ready to heal from the inside, on a deep level. Honestly, I didn't know where to start. I felt lost, confused and closed off at this point. But somehow, I knew it was time for me to really dive back into my past and heal. It wasn't just the relationship with Shane I needed healing from, it was going to take a lot more than that. I had to go right back to the beginning. It was time to remember my *entire* story, and it was time to learn how to heal from it, so I didn't keep slipping back into the habit of self-numbing. Because that is exactly what I was doing.

I was drowning my feelings in alcohol, cigarettes and, as much as I hate to admit it, I was snorting cocaine so I wouldn't have to feel the hurt. I was slipping into old habits again, and this was dangerous. This was the first moment I realised what self-numbing was, and the first time I recognised what I was doing. I am fucking better than this! Between my hair falling out and my self-numbing behaviours, it really scared the absolute shit out of me!

What the fuck was I doing? This really gave me the push I needed to do something about it. I chose ME and, if the people around me did not support that decision, I was at the point where I did not care—I was happy to let anyone go if I had to. The time had come to put me first. And this meant I had to feel EVERYTHING:

- NO MORE SELF NUMBING
- NO MORE PUTTING OTHERS BEFORE ME
- NO MORE EMOTIONLESS RELATIONSHIPS
- NO MORE REPEATING ANY PAST MISTAKES
- NO MORE SUGAR-COATING OTHER PEOPLE'S SHIT!

Around this time, I kept stumbling across a page on social media for Tess, an Intuitive Coach, Author, and Psychic Medium, and I felt drawn to her and the work she does: reiki, readings, and private coaching. Eventually I reached out and booked a *Reiki & Reading* session with her. I was nervous and, honestly, I had no expectations walking into her space for the first time. I just knew I *had* to start somewhere on my healing journey, before it was too late and my entire being shut down. I mean, I was already dangerously close to this happening.

The session was absolutely amazing! Tess made me feel comfortable in her space. My psychic reading was filled with people who loved me, and angels that I believe have kept me safe and alive throughout this journey of mine. The reiki was so powerful that during the next few weeks I felt clear and focused while at work. I knew I needed to continue my journey with this amazing woman, so I reached out to her again, and we chatted about private coaching.

The thing that really grabbed me was that Tess worked on healing from the inside out. She was caring and genuine and I loved how secure I felt in her space. Throughout the three months of the coaching phase, Tess focused on healing my soul on a deeper level. We delved deep into the past and present traumas that continued to come back and haunt me. Releasing old patterns and working within the body to release any blockages.

This course marked the end of my tragic story and a new beginning of living and loving *me* for the first time. I have gone from being closed off with social anxiety, having no periods, my hair falling out, drinking, smoking excessively, occasionally snorting cocaine, and with no direction in life to ... where I am now. I feel joy in my heart again, and I am confident in myself and in life. I wake each day and feel so grateful to be exactly where I am. My periods are finally back (I never thought I would be happy about that!) and my hair has stopped falling out.

And most of all I am doing all of this with absolutely no *substances* in my life. I knew I needed to feel every bit of emotion throughout the process. My body was healing, and it took me to finally choose *me* and do the work, for this to happen. I never understood how my past had affected my entire life. Now, I am not saying for one second that I will never have a drink again, but I do know I will *never* allow myself to self-numb again, and I will also *never* allow anyone to bring me to a point where I need to. We all have a breaking point, and this is what it took for me to make life-altering changes.

I know what my purpose is, and how I want to help others. And it is right here, doing what I am doing now ... writing this book to show you that we can change. Now I am not saying we all have the same story, but I will say that sometimes we have no control over the 'choices' we are forced to make. It is called survival mode for a reason, and it is the only way we can continue to live, until we choose not to.

And let me tell you, none of it easy! So please don't hate or judge those still in addiction, for they are not doing any of what they do at all consciously, or to hurt you. They are simply surviving each day the best way they know how to.

Speaking our truth is fucking scary but ... there is so much power in this. The healing journey I've been on throughout writing this book has been mind-blowing! It's taken courage to relive all of this, but at the same time I finally feel free.

Now it's time for me to help *you* speak *your* truth.

Chapter 13

Through these many months of really working on myself, my past, and all the shitty things that I have experienced on my life journey … my heart is now open and ready for my true love to enter my life. When it arrives of course, there is no hurry. A girl's allowed to have a little fun while she waits, right? Ha-ha! I know my fucking worth now, and I know what I want and what I deserve. I believe my last relationship gave me an experience of a different type of love, and it taught me to see and feel, on a soul level, how I want, need, and deserve to be loved. It was as if I mirrored myself to see and feel love on a whole new level.

I realised I had received everything I had asked for on the little list I wrote so many years ago. I had actually forgotten about it until the subject came up during my coaching. Tess and I had spoken about writing a list and asking the Universe for what I wanted. I remember thinking, *"OMG, I already have that list!"*, and then racing home to take a look at it. Every box was ticked!

- **NO MORE DEBT:** Which was my financial freedom
  - ○ **TICK!**
- **TRAVEL:** I'd had a few holidays overseas
  - ○ **TICK!**
- **THE RIGHT MAN:** A man who was financially stable and my best friend, and I'd had this, so
  - ○ **TICK!**

So, let me tell you, I tore that list up, grabbed a pen and a piece of paper and wrote down, in fine detail, exactly what I wanted and needed in a man. In great big letters, I wrote 'IF THEY ARE EMOTIONALLY UNAVAILABLE, PLEASE DO NOT SEND TO ME', along with a lot of other specifics.

How powerful is it to write stuff down?! I never realised it until that moment, seeing that the list I had written many, many, years ago was ticked off completely. How fucking powerful is this?!

I remember during one coaching session with Tess, what came through was that I would write a book. Let me tell you, when I heard this, I thought, *"My goodness, I could never do anything like that. Who would want to read my story?"*

I knew I wanted, *needed*, to remember my past, and to do that I was going to delve into a little writing in order for me to heal. But not for a second did I dream I would be sitting here now writing it for you, too. I have always wanted to help people; I had this urge inside me. I just never knew how, where to start, and what these feelings were.

For me my past was jumbled around in my head, and even going back and re-writing it was a little tricky. It was a challenge trying to piece it all together, especially after blocking out so much, and then learning to push past things. But that's okay, it's not meant to be perfect. It just needed to help me heal and show you that there is always hope, and that not all stories end badly.

It has been quite a journey and, at times, extremely heavy to write, and even heavier to read back to myself. I learnt to put it down and walk away when it got to that point, until I was ready to come back to it. But, as hard as it has been, writing my story has been empowering. Delving back into everything and truly allowing myself to sit with it and, most of all, forgiving myself and the people who hurt me—this is where the power lies.

I have learnt to *recognise* behaviours that are not okay—mine and other people's—and to stop *excusing* other people's unacceptable behaviours. I learnt to recognise and accept that I was raped, that I was emotionally abused, and that my light and life was stolen from me. Previously, I could never really bring myself to say, "I was raped", because I always had this image in my mind that rape was brutally violent. So, I fluffed it up, I diminished it by saying, "I was taken advantage of". But this was not the brutal truth.

So, you see the turning point for me was my relationship with Shane. It literally took me breaking AGAIN, and self-numbing AGAIN, to get me to my 'WHAT THE FUCK AM I DOING?' moment, to want to finally heal myself on a deeper level. As shitty as the relationship was sometimes, I am so fucking grateful for it. And, once again, I wouldn't change one damn piece of my story. I am not saying my life is perfect, but I know some things for sure: I will *never* self-numb again, I will *never* be silenced again, and I will allow myself to feel whatever I need to without judging myself for it.

My name is Bianca Ozzimo, and now you know my name and just some of my story. With some of the experiences I lived through, I probably shouldn't be alive, but I am, and I was meant to share my journey with you.

I am a survivor of rape

I am a survivor of drug addiction

I am a survivor of attempted suicide

I am a survivor of mental abuse

I am a survivor of emotional abuse

I am a survivor of self-abuse

... and I am a warrior woman who has sat here and re-lived all of those moments so I can forgive anyone who ever hurt me, including myself. Most importantly, I have allowed myself to fall in love with ME for the very first time.

I believe that if I can do all of this, so can you or your loved ones. I hope my story gives you hope, strength, and the courage to speak your truth—the story that you have been silenced from telling all these years, so that you too can become free. And I also hope it gives you the permission to make choices to help you step into your true self, and who you are meant to be. Always remember this ... **'it is happening FOR you, not TO you'**, even when it may not feel this way, you will look back one day, and you will see it clearly.

Thank you so much for reading my book to the end, I will be forever grateful that you did. I hope one day I will hear from you, so I can help you to speak your truth and learn to let go of guilt, hate, shame and blame.

You will never understand the power that exists in allowing yourself to speak your truth, until you take that first, fearful step to DO IT. So, what are you waiting for? Push your fear aside and start living for YOU!

About the Author

BIANCA OZZIMO

Victim. Survivor. Advocate.

Bianca Ozzimo is one of those rare individuals who has successfully made the transition from victim to survivor to advocate to improve the lives of others. As a result of her own life experience, she is passionate about helping others speak their truth to help them become free from past traumas and addictions through the power of writing, Reiki and sound healing.

By necessity, her style is raw, authentic and uncompromising, however, Bianca is also a creative soul who brings truth and beauty to everything she does.

Bianca lives in Queensland, Australia, on the beautiful Gold Coast where she now practices as an alternative and holistic healer.

Expect to hear more from Bianca Ozzimo.

Acknowledgements

To my angel, my grandfather, my Pop who was taken from me too soon. I truly believe you have been right by my side every step of the way. I wouldn't be here today if it was not for you lifting me up and lighting the way for me through the dark. Guiding me to exactly where I am now to become the light for others. Thank you, and I love you so very much.

To my S.S., my sassy sister ... Kelle Dee. You came back into my life right before I became a million broken pieces. Thank you so much for being right by my side through all the 'shitty times' and then supporting me every step of the way through this journey. You have been my absolute rock and I am so grateful to have you in my life. Thank you for not only loving me on my good days, but for loving me that little extra on my darkest days when I felt I couldn't get through the next 24 hours. I am so grateful to have you in my life, thank you so much, and I love you dearly. Life would sparkle less without you in it! xo

To the beautiful Jess Sermak. Being guided to you was an absolute blessing and it has honestly changed my life. None of what is happening right now would be possible without your support and guidance—not even this book. The first time I met you I was so closed off, lost, and near broken. You held a safe space for me where I was seen, heard, and understood. You believed in me and all I had to offer this world, even when I did not believe in myself. I am forever thankful and grateful for you. Thank you, beautiful soul sister.

To my wonderful publisher Deborah Fay, Disruptive Publishing. Deb you are such a gentle soul. From our very first meeting you were so kind, understanding and, most of all, patient. I changed my mind a few times, I had so much self-doubt and you just held that safe space for me until I was ready to go. You really took the time to listen to what I wanted and picked the perfect team, including yourself, to make my book happen from the editing process to printing. I am so very grateful for you, and none of this would be possible without you. Thank you so much

To my absolutely amazing editor, Jo Scott. What can I say, but WOW! Working with you throughout the entire editing process has been incredible. You really made it pain-free, exciting, and enjoyable. Thank you for keeping my story true to my own words. Keeping it real and raw was exactly what I wanted for my readers, and you really listened to me and did exactly that. Throughout this process I have begun to actually enjoy reading my own story, FINALLY. This would never have been possible without all of your amazing work. Thank you so much.

To my family, and my nearest and dearest friends who I now call family, thank you for supporting me through the lows and the highs of this massive journey of life. Life would not be the same without each and every one of you. You all know who you are, and I hold so much love in my heart for you. Each one of you adds a little something different to my life, and I love you all very dearly. Thank you.

More from BIANCA

Journey with Bee
An alternative and holistic health service, creating a safe space for women to *speak their truth*

Bianca offers healing and recovery strategies, including:

- *Reiki and sound healing*
- *Women's circle facilitator*
- *Group sound healings*

What's next from BIANCA

Upcoming publications:

Let me help you speak your truth
—*A compilation of men and women's stories*

Connect with BIANCA

Facebook: Journey with Bee
facebook.com/search/top?q=journey%20with%20bee

Email: journeywithbe3@gmail.com

Testimonials

What does it really mean to genuinely survive; to not just pull through from grimly excruciating experiences, but to actually make meaning of your life and help others? Bianca vividly answers that question as she lays bare her wretched young life and leads her readers to a new understanding of what it means to face your demons, survive that confrontation, reconcile oneself, and thrive afterwards! This raw and heartbreakingly honest book is more than a cautionary tale, it is a ray of hope for those who have been crushed by addictive abuses.

Matthew C.
Military Survival Instructor

You Know My Name … Not My Story will have you captivated right from the very first page as Bianca shares with us the reality of what it's like to struggle with a long term drug addiction and the deep shame, embarrassment, and fear that often comes with that

Bianca offers up such vulnerability in her story as she speaks the truth of what happened to her that led her down the addiction path and the trauma and abuse that followed. You Know My Name … Not My Story is one of the most raw, real, and relatable books you will ever read!

Bianca's empowering message is clear that behind every addiction is a story, often a very painful story that keeps the person in addiction feeling trapped by an inner belief that something is wrong with them. Seeking substances and things to numb and comfort the deep pain. However, Bianca helps us to see that we are asking the wrong questions, it's not about what's wrong with an addict, rather it's about asking what happened to them ...

Bianca's book offers anyone who has ever struggled with addiction hope, whether it be drugs, alcohol, smoking, sex, or shopping. Hope that there is life after addiction as long as they courageously speak their truth and give themselves the gift of self-forgiveness as they explore what happened to them.

This beautiful book teaches us that each of us has a choice: we can sugar-coat it and tell ourselves we are fine as we spiral into our addictions and pain **or** *we can courageously speak our truth, liberate our voices, and illuminate what is really going on for us.*

If you have stumbled across this inspirational book trust that it's for a big reason, may it speak to your soul, illuminate your story and give you the hope you need to courageously speak your truth!

Jess Sermak
Author, *Becoming a Butterfly*

Bianca tells her story in a way that is so raw, interesting, real, and inspirational, I struggled to put it down. A lot of her story really resonated with me and helped me to remember parts of **my** *life that I had chosen to forget; remembering has helped me to do more healing within myself. Thank you, Bianca.*

Karen Brown
Zen Reiki Healing

Congratulations to Bianca for having the courage to share her story. I was totally immersed in it and on the edge of my seat as she related every step of her journey. This is a story that needed to be told.

Rita-Marie Lenton
Author, *Creating a Fond Farewell*

I could not put it down and read it in one sitting! It's great to read how Bianca triumphed after all that she endured. What an inspirational story about learning to love yourself. Being blessed by Angels in those life-defining moments is wonderful.

Albina Porracin
Author, *Help Me – My Finances Are a Mess!*

Bianca shows great self-awareness and shares her story from a position of power, and her story touched me emotionally throughout.

Raw, real, and remarkable—what a wonderful insight Bianca has given through her strength and courage. Her story empowers others as she shines a light on her journey, stating her purpose with clarity, strength, and compassion; the energy of her words is palpable.

This book has the potential to touch many lives.

Di Riddell
Author, *Speak Out*

www.ingramcontent.com/pod-product-compliance
Lightning Source LLC
Chambersburg PA
CBHW060806110426
42739CB00032BA/3114